# CHRISTMAS
# EVE

ISBN 978-0-7935-3787-7

HAL•LEONARD™
CORPORATION

7777 W. BLUEMOUND RD. P.O. BOX 13819 MILWAUKEE, WI 53213

Cover artist photo by Rosanne Olson
CD cover illustration by Rick Thrun/Marx, McClellan & Thrun; Inside artist photo by Rob v. Uchelen
Design by Connie Gage and Wesley Van Linda

NP-90011SB

# CHRISTMAS
# EVE

◆

## TABLE OF CONTENTS

| | |
|---|---|
| A Brush of Wings | 53 |
| An Angel at Midnight | 62 |
| The Angel King | 27 |
| Angel of Comfort | 5 |
| Angel of Hope | 44 |
| Angel of Joy | 19 |
| Angels We Have Heard on High | 6 |
| The First Noël/Christmas Eve Waltz | 28 |
| God Rest Ye Merry Gentlemen | 14 |
| "I Saw the Path of the Angels" | 63 |
| Joy to the World | 34 |
| O Come All Ye Faithful | 20 |
| O Come, O Come, Emmanuel | 46 |
| O Holy Night | 74 |
| O Little Town of Bethlehem | 40 |
| Silent Night | 66 |
| What Child is This | 54 |

# CHRISTMAS EVE

Winter is the time when Mother Earth takes a breath inward, and I believe it very natural for us to pause and do the same — to allow ourselves time for introspection amidst all the celebration and activity of the holidays. The music on CHRISTMAS EVE was created during such a time in my own life.

Though the arrangements for some of these carols and the idea for the album began in the Winter of 1990, most of the work and all of the recording occurred at home during an "extended Christmas respite" that followed a very rigorous touring schedule during most of 1993.

As the work progressed and each carol developed from fragments and wisps to finished works, I imagined that an Angel, a Guardian Angel of sorts, existed for each of the songs. These Angels seemed to guide my hand and heart throughout the process. They also resulted in the seven Angel Improvisations threaded between the carols. Musical inward breaths.

If the music encourages your own quiet introspections, that was my hope and intention. This mood is surely the very essence of the spirit of the holiday. But if you do take that inward breath, don't be surprised if you feel a light brush of Angel wings and hear the softest of whispers . . . .

Wishing you peace and God's blessings,

*David Lanz*

*"Above the deep and dreamless sleep, the silent stars go by."*

# ANGEL OF COMFORT

Composed by
DAVID LANZ

Slow

With pedal

# ANGELS WE HAVE HEARD ON HIGH

Arranged by
DAVID LANZ

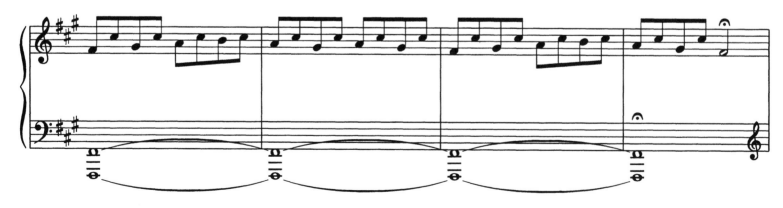

R.H. over L.H.

# GOD REST YE MERRY GENTLEMEN

Arranged by
DAVID LANZ

With motion

*mp*

With pedal

R.H.

# ANGEL OF JOY

Composed by
DAVID LANZ

# O COME ALL YE FAITHFUL

Arranged by
DAVID LANZ

**Moderately**

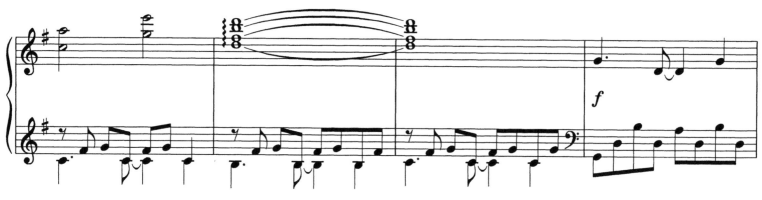

# THE ANGEL KING

Composed by
DAVID LANZ

# THE FIRST NOËL/
# CHRISTMAS EVE WALTZ

Composed and Arranged by
DAVID LANZ

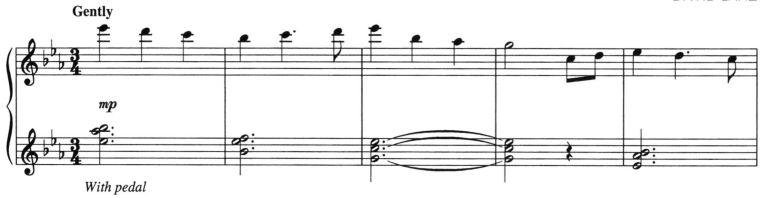

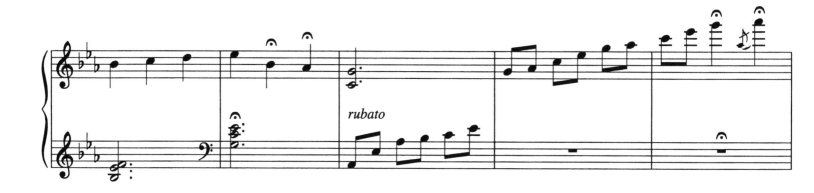

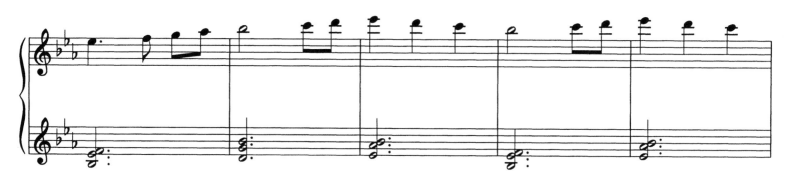

# JOY TO THE WORLD

Arranged by
DAVID LANZ

Briskly

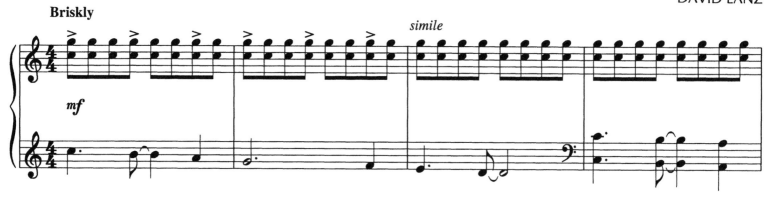

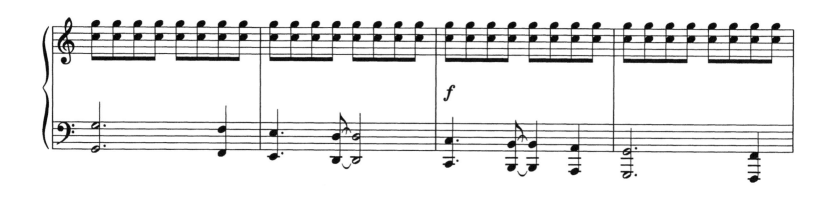

35

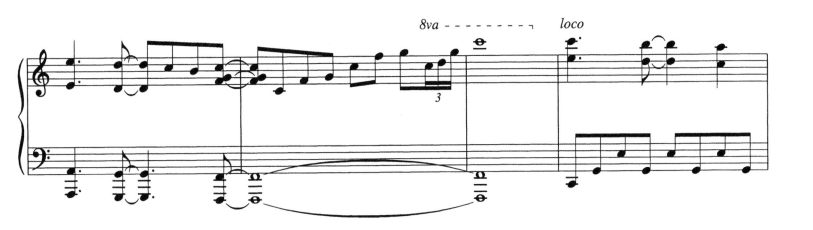

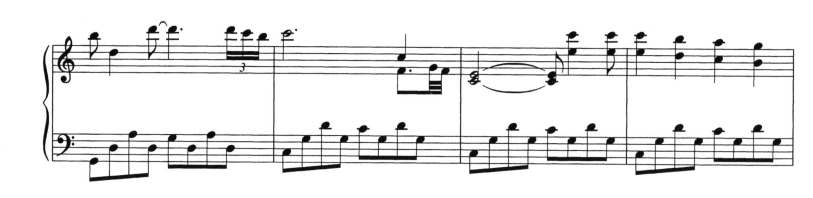

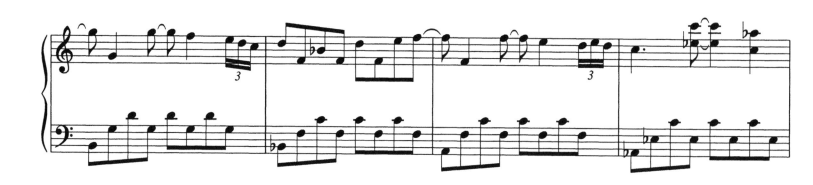

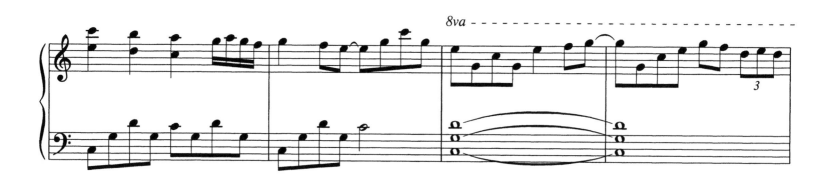

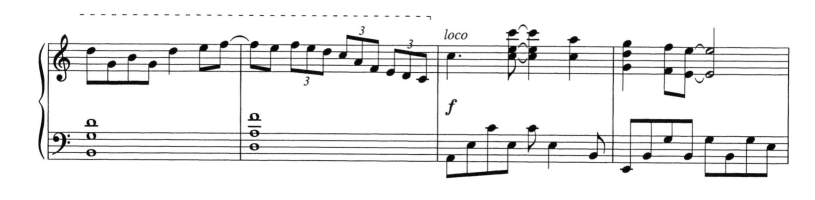

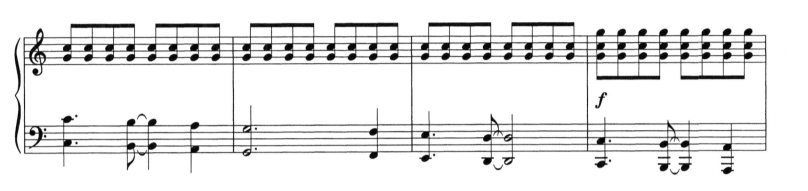

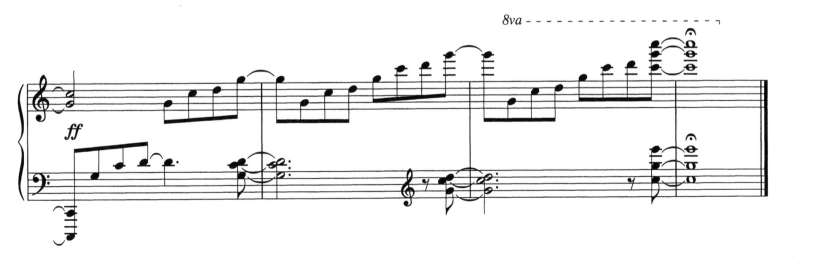

# O LITTLE TOWN OF BETHLEHEM

Arranged by
DAVID LANZ

# ANGEL OF HOPE

Composed by
DAVID LANZ

# O COME, O COME, EMMANUEL

Arranged by
DAVID LANZ

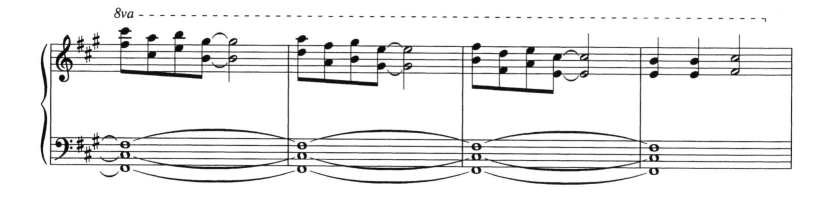

**Moderately**

*rit.*   *mp*   *a tempo*

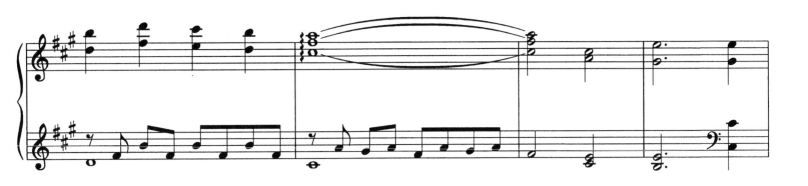

50

# A BRUSH OF WINGS

Composed by
DAVID LANZ

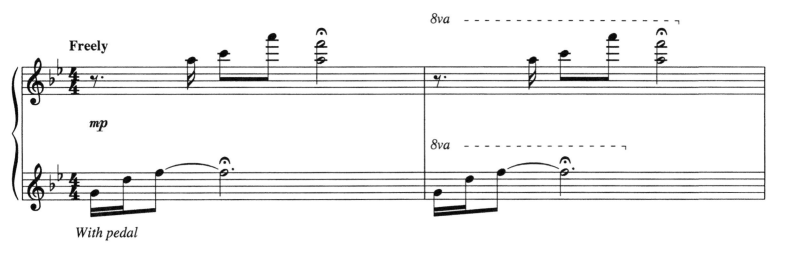

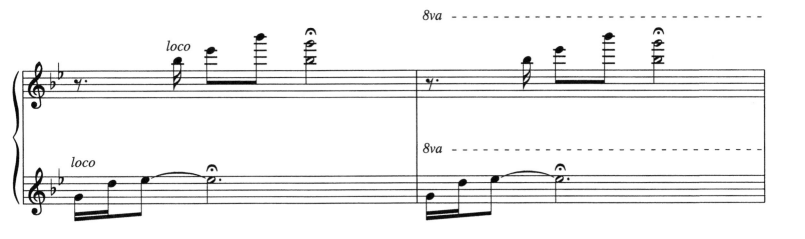

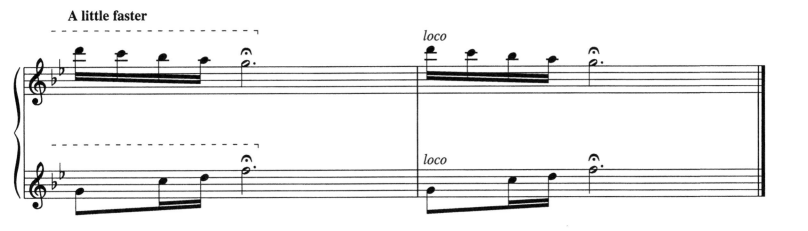

# WHAT CHILD IS THIS

Arranged by
DAVID LANZ

**Gently**

*mp*

*With pedal*

*R.H.*

*R.H.*

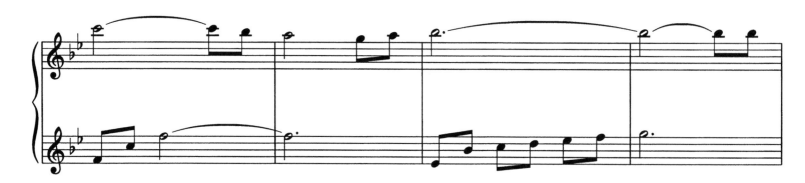

# AN ANGEL AT MIDNIGHT

Composed by
DAVID LANZ

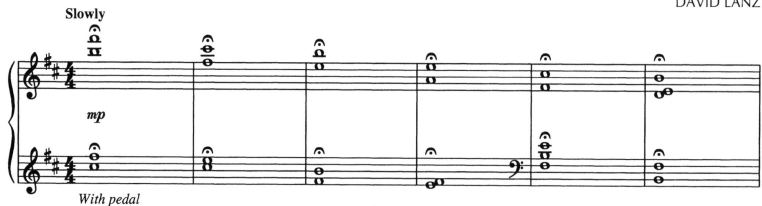

# "I SAW THE PATH OF THE ANGELS"

Composed by DAVID LANZ

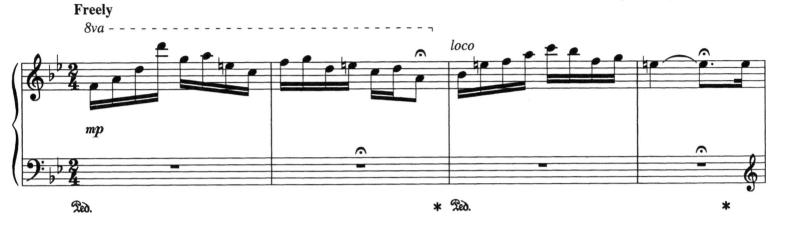

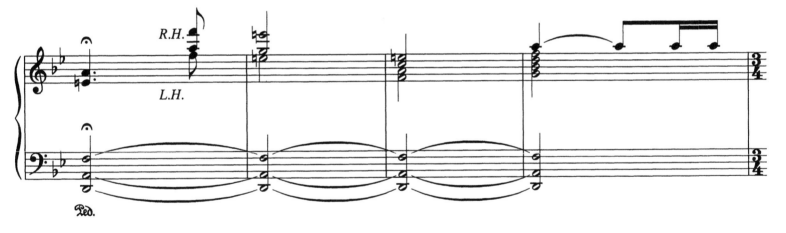

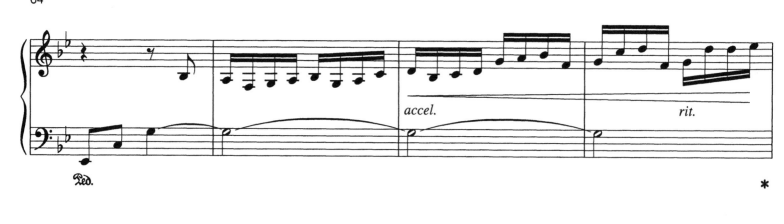

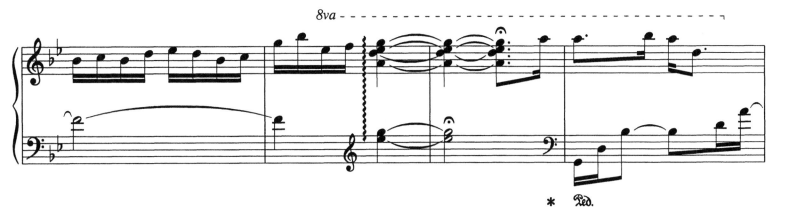

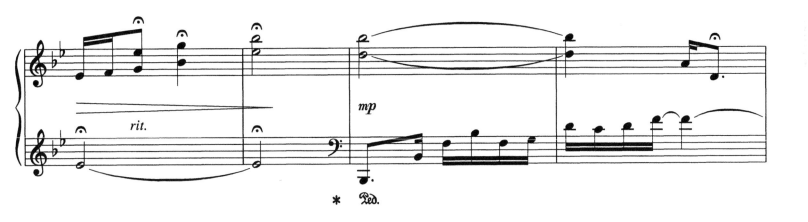

# SILENT NIGHT

Arranged by
DAVID LANZ

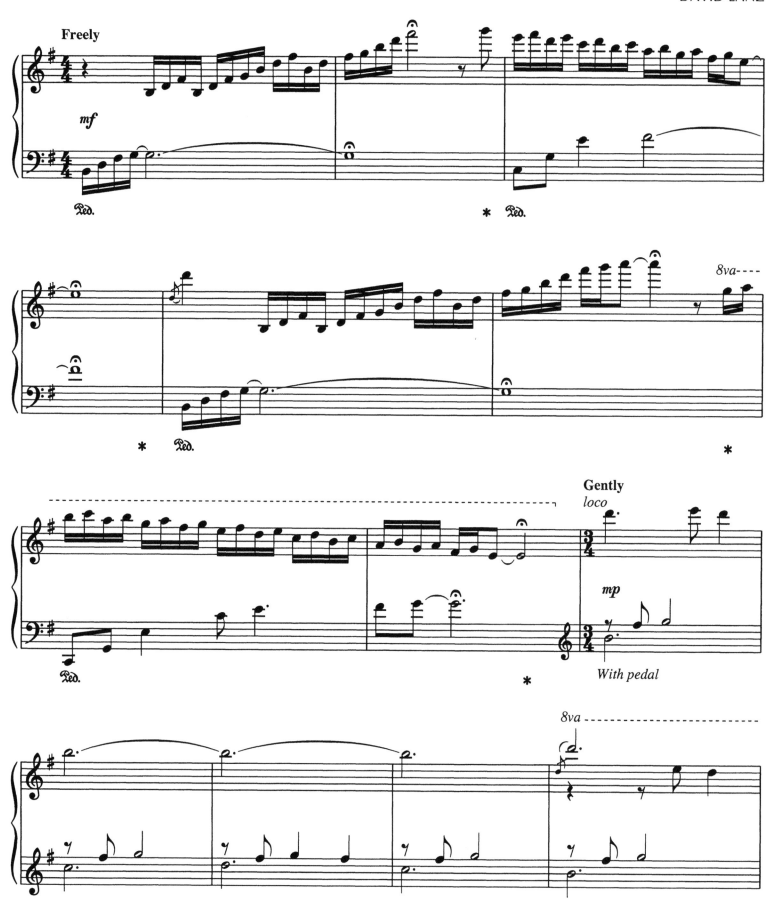

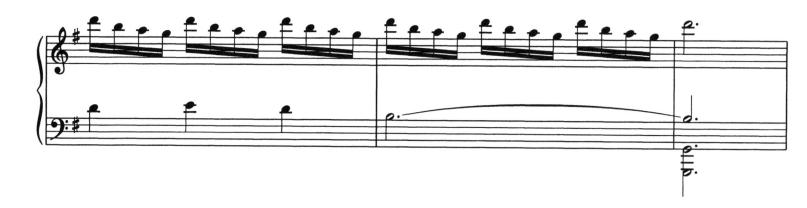

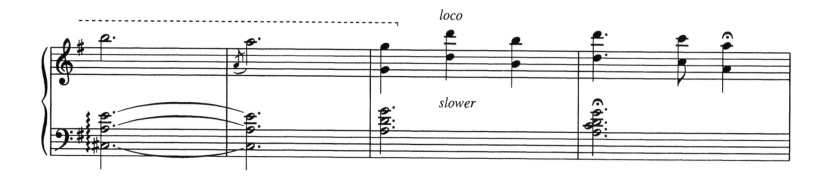

# O HOLY NIGHT

Arranged by
DAVID LANZ

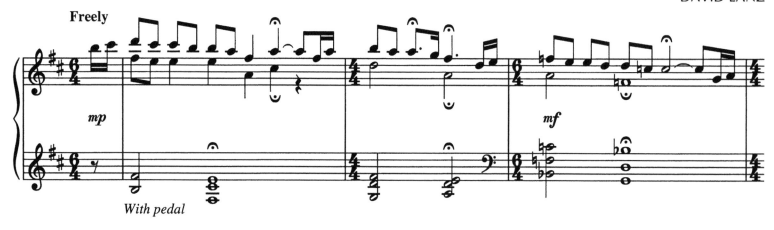

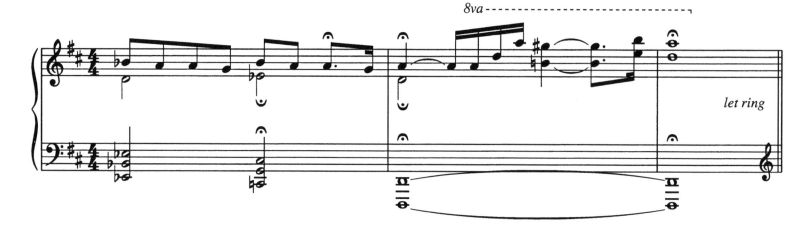

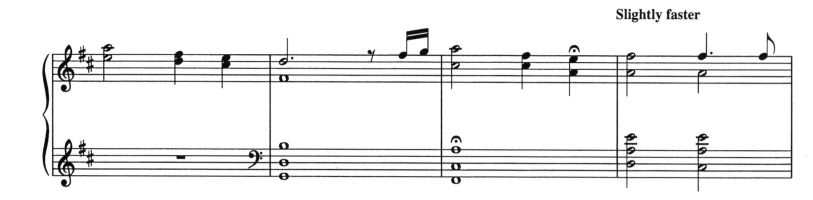

A little faster

# A CATALOG OF NARADA RECORDINGS

## NARADA LOTUS — New Acoustic Music

| | |
|---|---|
| N-61001 | PIANOSCAPES  Michael Jones |
| N-61002 | SEASONS  Gabriel Lee |
| N-61003 | HEARTSOUNDS  David Lanz |
| N-61004 | SEASCAPES  Michael Jones |
| N-61005 | IMPRESSIONS  Gabriel Lee |
| N-61006 | NIGHTFALL  David Lanz |
| N-61007 | SAMPLER 1  Narada Artists |
| N-61008 | SOLSTICE  Jones and Lanz |
| N-61009 | SUNSCAPES  Michael Jones |
| N-61010 | OPENINGS  William Ellwood |
| N-61011 | EMERALD  Tingstad, Rumbel and Brewer |
| N-61012 | QUIET FIRE  Ancient Future |
| N-61013 | SAMPLER 2  Narada Artists |
| N-61014 | AMBER  Jones and Darling |
| N-61015 | RENAISSANCE  William Ellwood |
| N-61016 | WOODLANDS  Tingstad, Rumbel and Lanz |
| N-61017 | PORTRAITS  Spencer Brewer |
| N-61018 | SAMPLER 3  Narada Artists |
| N-61019 | DEPARTURES  John Doan |
| N-61020 | AFTER THE RAIN  Michael Jones |
| N-61021 | CRISTOFORI'S DREAM  David Lanz |
| N-61022 | LEGENDS  Eric Tingstad and Nancy Rumbel |
| N-61023 | REMINISCENCE  Wayne Gratz |
| N-61024 | VISTA  William Ellwood |
| N-61025 | SAMPLER 4  Narada Artists |
| N-61026 | HOMELAND  Eric Tingstad and Nancy Rumbel |
| N-61027 | MAGICAL CHILD  Michael Jones |
| N-61028 | PANORAMA  Wayne Gratz |
| N-61029 | WISDOM OF THE WOOD  Narada Artists |
| N-61030 | MORNING IN MEDONTE  Michael Jones |
| N-61031 | PIANO SOLOS  Narada Artists |
| N-61032 | GUITAR WORKS  Narada Artists |
| N-61033 | CAROUSEL  Ira Stein |
| N-61034 | FOLLOW ME HOME  Wayne Gratz |
| N-61035 | ROMANTIC INTERLUDES  Spencer Brewer |
| N-61036 | GIVE AND TAKE  Eric Tingstad and Nancy Rumbel |
| N-61037 | WIND AND REED  Narada Artists |
| N-61038 | TOUSHSTONE  William Ellwood |
| N-61039 | SIMON  Simon Wynberg |
| N-61040 | SUITE ST. PETERSBURG  Kostia |
| N-61041 | NARADA LOTUS ACOUSTIC SAMPLER 5  Narada Artists |
| N-61042 | AIR BORN  Michael Jones |
| N-61043 | STAR OF WONDER  Eric Tingstad and Nancy Rumbel |
| N-61044 | PASSION - MUSIC FOR GUITAR  Narada Artists |
| N-61045 | ROMANCE - MUSIC FOR PIANO  Various Artists |
| N-61046 | CHRISTMAS EVE  David Lanz |

## NARADA MYSTIQUE — New Electronic Music

| | |
|---|---|
| N-62001 | VALLEY IN THE CLOUDS  David Arkenstone |
| N-62002 | THE WAITING  Peter Buffett |
| N-62003 | HIDDEN PATHWAYS  Bruce Mitchell |
| N-62004 | ONE BY ONE  Peter Buffett |
| N-62005 | A VIEW FROM THE BRIDGE  Carol Nethen |
| N-62006 | INTRUDING ON A SILENCE  Colin Chin |
| N-62007 | DANCING ON THE EDGE  Bruce Mitchell |
| N-62008 | CITIZEN OF TIME  David Arkenstone |
| N-62009 | MYSTIQUE SAMPLER ONE  Narada Artists |
| N-62010 | WARM SOUND IN A GRAY FIELD  Peter Maunu |
| N-62011 | THE MESSENGER  Jim Jacobsen |
| N-62012 | LOST FRONTIER  Peter Buffett |
| N-62013 | YONNONDIO  Peter Buffett |
| N-62014 | ANOTHER STAR IN THE SKY  David Arkenstone |

## NARADA EQUINOX — Crossover/Jazz/World

| | |
|---|---|
| N-63001 | NATURAL STATES  David Lanz and Paul Speer |
| N-63002 | INDIAN SUMMER  Friedemann |
| N-63003 | DESERT VISION  David Lanz and Paul Speer |
| N-63004 | EQUINOX SAMPLER ONE  Narada Artists |
| N-63005 | ISLAND  David Arkenstone with Andrew White |
| N-63006 | CIRCLE  Ralf Illenberger |
| N-63007 | CROSS CURRENTS  Richard Souther |
| N-63008 | DORIAN'S LEGACY  Spencer Brewer |
| N-63009 | HEART & BEAT  Ralf Illenberger |
| N-63010 | MIL AMORES  Doug Cameron |
| N-63011 | MOON RUN  Trapezoid |
| N-63012 | CAFÉ DU SOLEIL  Brian Mann |
| N-63013 | WHITE LIGHT  Martin Kolbe |
| N-63014 | NEW LAND  Bernardo Rubaja |
| N-63015 | TWELVE TRIBES  Richard Souther |
| N-63016 | EQUINOX SAMPLER TWO  Narada Artists |
| N-63017 | AQUAMARINE  Friedemann |
| N-63018 | THE PIPER'S RHYTHM  Spencer Brewer |
| N-63019 | PLACES IN TIME  Michael Gettel |
| N-63020 | JOURNEY TO YOU  Doug Cameron |
| N-63021 | SOLEIL  Ralf Illenberger |
| N-63022 | RHYTHM HARVEST  The Michael Pluznick Group |
| N-63023 | ASIAN FUSION  Ancient Future |
| N-63024 | BRIDGE OF DREAMS  David Lanz and Paul Speer |
| N-63025 | SKYWATCHING  Michael Gettel |
| N-63026 | PONITS OF VIEW  Nando Lauria |
| N-63027 | THE KEY  Michael Gettel |
| N-63028 | LIQUID SMOKE  Randy Roos |
| N-63029 | SPUR OF THE MOMENT  Ira Stein Group |
| N-63030 | ARCTIC BLUE  Peter Rodgers Melnick |

## NARADA COLLECTION SERIES

| | |
|---|---|
| N-39100 | NARADA COLLECTION 1  Narada Artists |
| N-39117 | NARADA COLLECTION 2  Narada Artists |
| N-63902 | NARADA CHRISTMAS COLLECTION  Narada Artists |
| N-63904 | THE NARADA NUTCRACKER  Narada Artists |
| N-63905 | THE NARADA WILDERNESS COLLECTION  Narada Artists |
| N-63906 | NARADA COLLECTION 3  Narada Artists |
| N-63907 | A CHILDHOOD REMEMBERED  Narada Artists |
| N-63908 | ALMA DEL SUR  Various Artists |
| N-63909 | NARADA CHRISTMAS COLLECTION VOLUME 2  Narada Artists |
| N-63910 | NARADA COLLECTION 4  Narada Artists |
| N-63911 | NARADA DECADE  Narada Artists |
| N-63912 | CELTIC ODYSSEY  Various Artists |
| N-63913 | EARTH SONGS  Narada Artists |
| N-63914 | THE SOUND OF LIGHT  Various Artists |

## THE NARADA ARTIST SERIES

| | |
|---|---|
| N-64001 | SKYLINE FIREDANCE  David Lanz |
| N-64002 | MICHAEL'S MUSIC  Michael Jones |
| N-64003 | IN THE WAKE OF THE WIND  David Arkenstone |
| N-64004 | IN THE GARDEN  Eric Tingstad and Nancy Rumbel |
| N-64005 | RETURN TO THE HEART  David Lanz |
| N-64006 | THE SPIRIT OF OLYMPIA  Arkenstone, Kostia, Lanz |
| N-64007 | CHRONICLES  David Arkenstone |

## NARADA CINEMA

| | |
|---|---|
| N-66001 | MILLENNIUM: TRIBAL WISDOM AND THE MODERN WORLD  Hans Zimmer |
| N-66002 | COLUMBUS AND THE AGE OF DISCOVERY  Sheldon Mirowitz |
| N-66003 | SPACE AGE  Jay Chattaway |
| N-66004 | THE DINOSAURS!  Peter Rodgers Melnick |
| N-66005 | SEAPOWER: A GLOBAL JOURNEY  Michael Whalen |
| N-66006 | GREAT AFRICAN MOMENTS  Michael Whalen |
| N-66007 | PHANTOM OF THE FOREST  Michael Whalen |
| N-66008 | KUNG FU: THE LEGEND CONTINUES  Jeff Danna |

Narada appreciates the support of its listeners, and we welcome your comments about the music of our artists.
Narada publishes a free, semi-annual newsletter that features information on new recordings.
You may receive future copies by writing to us and joining our worldwide family of quality-minded listeners.

Please write to: Friends of Narada, 4650 N. Port Washington Road., Milwaukee, WI 53212-1063 USA, or
Friends of Narada, P.O. Box 2301, 1200 CH Hilversum, Netherlands.